Story©Kimm Reid

Illustrations©Taralee Tilma

All rights reserved. No part of this work covered by the copyrights hereon may be reproduced or used in any form or by any means—graphic, electronic, or mechanical—without the prior written permission of the publisher, including both the story and the illustrations.

ISBN: 978-1-998243-27-3

visit me @ kimm reid.org

visit us @ aheliapublishing.com

Published in Montana, USA

Printed in the USA

It's OK to Cry

BY KIMM REID

(WIH THE HELP OF SWEET ANNABELLE)

ILLUSTRATED BY TARALEE TILMA

i am SAD

I was so sad, I started to cry. My brother laughed at me, but I didn't care. My heart was sad, and it made tears sneak out of my eyes. I was playing with my favorite dolly, Annabelle, when my sister pulled her from my hands and ran out of the house. I chased her down the stairs, but I couldn't catch up. My sister is bigger than me and can run faster. She took sweet Annabelle and threw her into a tree so high that I couldn't reach to get her down.

It made my heart hurt, and I cried for a long time. I thought I might never stop crying. I was so sad.

When my dad got home, he climbed up the tree and rescued Annabelle. I think she was sad too, but when I hugged her, she whispered to me.

"It's ok to be sad—I'm sad too. If something hurts your heart, you must let it be sad for a while but don't give sadness any power. It can feel like your heart might break into a hundred pieces, so it's ok to let it hurt. It's ok to cry—but don't cry forever.

Don't let sadness be stronger than your heart. Sadness can visit, but do not let it move in."

You own your SAD~
Your SAD doesn't own you.

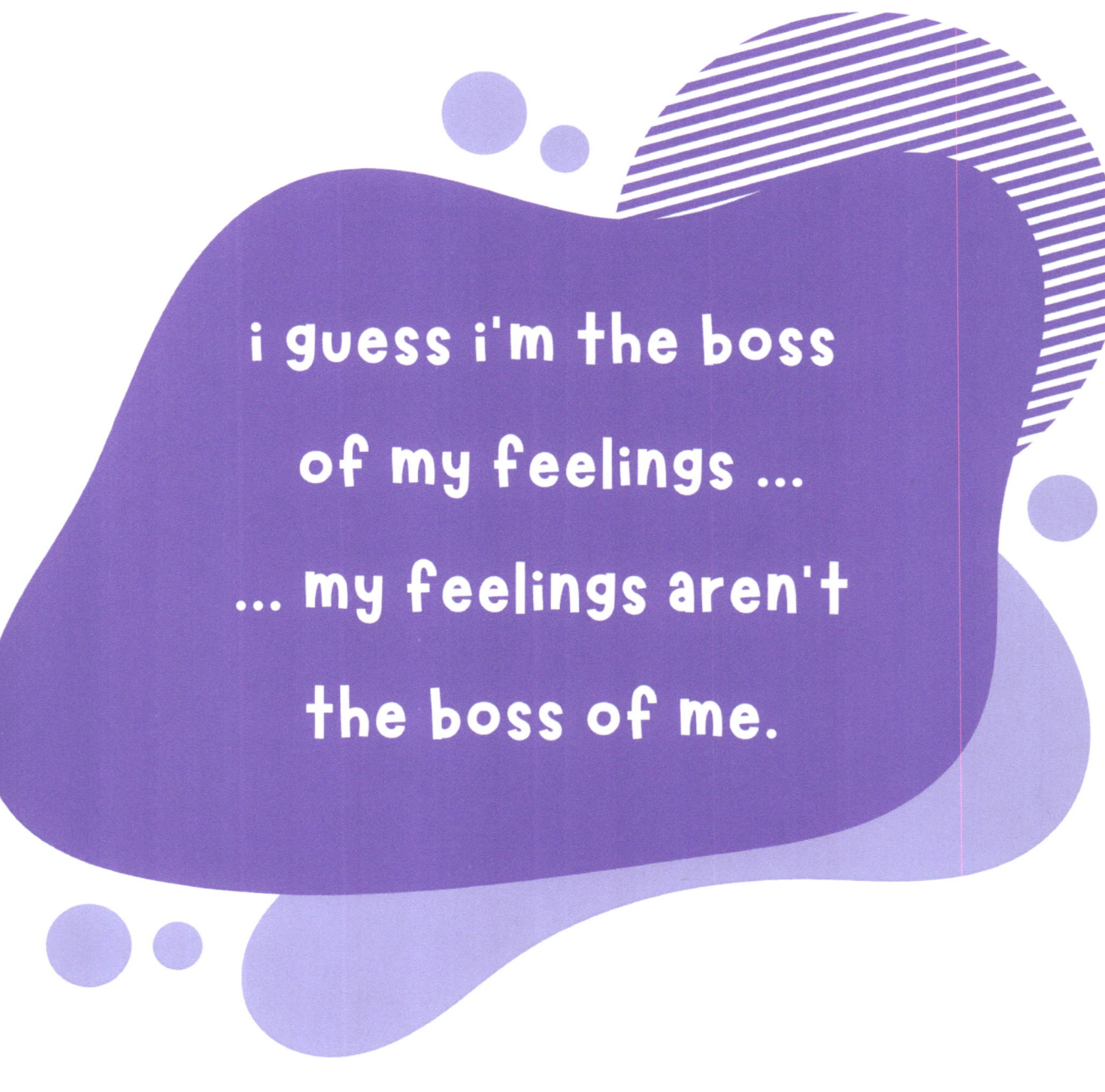

So, as Annabelle said, I let my heart feel sad for a little while because, after all, my sweet dolly was all messed up from being in the tree. I straightened her dress and combed her hair, but she still had some smudges on her face and a rip in her bow.

I felt sad for a few more minutes but then told the sadness it had to go. It couldn't have more power than me! I sniffled.

I wiped my nose and dried my eyes. I started singing the happiest song I knew and danced around with Annabelle.

If she could be happy, then I could be happy too.

I *chose* to be happy.
I *chose* to forgive my sister for being mean.
I *chose* to forgive my brother for laughing at me.

I said,

"SAD, you cannot stay.
You visited my heart, but now it's time to go."

Goodbye, SAD.

i am MAD

I was so mad, my head almost exploded! My friend Violet said she would meet me at the park. My mom said I could go, so Annabelle and I pulled on our sneakers and ran to the park. We were so excited— Violet was one of our favorite friends!

Well, not anymore.

When Annabelle and I were running to the park, we saw Violet and Genevieve riding bikes. I waved, but Violet didn't stop. She didn't wave. She didn't go to the park. I guess she was having more fun with her new friend.

I guess Violet lied.

I stomped all the way home and threw Annabelle on my bed. I was so angry. I threw her too hard, and she slid onto the floor. I ran to pick her up, but I was still so angry.

"I'm sorry, Annabelle," I said. Now I felt angry at Violet for making me hurt Annabelle.

But Annabelle whispered back,

"Violet didn't make you throw me. You chose to do that because you were mad at her.

Sometimes it's hard to make good decisions when you're mad. Sometimes it's hard to remember we are mad at one person, and we become mean to another person.

It's ok to be mad. I'm mad, too! Violet told you a lie. She didn't want to play with you today. She should have told you the truth. Maybe she had already planned to ride bikes with Genevieve—you don't know. Maybe she didn't know how to do both things.

Anyway, being mad is ok when someone tells you a lie. You can be angry and even feel like being mean back.
But don't. Don't let mad stay.
Don't give mad your power.

Mad can visit you, but do not let it move in."

You own your MAD~ your MAD doesn't own you.

So I straightened her dress and smoothed her hair, but sweet Annabelle still looked a mess.

Maybe that's what mad looks like—a big mess.

I felt mad for a few more minutes but told mad it couldn't stay—it couldn't have any more power.

I blinked my eyes hard until they stung. Mad was stubborn; it didn't want to go. I sighed, started singing the happiest song I knew, and danced around with Annabelle.

If she could be happy, then I could be happy too.

I was mad for the whole day. Annabelle reminded me that mad had to go. It couldn't be stronger than me. So, I thought about it. I wanted the mad to stay. It made me feel good to be mad.

Violet hurt my feelings, and I liked being mad at her. She deserved it.

But Annabelle was right.

Maybe Violet forgot she was going to meet me. Maybe she didn't know what time it was. Maybe she was with Genevieve because Genevive was new to town and didn't have many friends. Maybe she didn't see me. I knew mad was only hurting me and Annabelle. After all, I threw her on the bed, and she fell to the floor.

I gave mad too much power and ended up hurting Annabelle.

I *chose* to be happy.
I *chose* to forgive Violet for not keeping her promise.
I *chose* to forgive Genevieve for taking my friend's time.
I told Annabelle I was sorry for throwing her on the bed.

I said,

"Mad, you cannot stay. You visited my mind,
but now you gotta go."

Goodbye, MAD.

i am AFRAID

I was so afraid that I could hardly move. My tongue felt weird. My mom and dad said goodnight hours ago, and I was supposed to be sleeping.
But it was dark, and I was scared of the dark.
I didn't know what was hiding in the dark.
When it was dark, everything was loud.

Noises I didn't hear in the light seemed loud in the dark. I didn't know what was in the closet. I didn't know what was under the bed. I got a little sweaty, and I was afraid to close my eyes.

I couldn't go to sleep when I was so afraid. I kept trying hard to keep my eyes open, even though I couldn't see. Even when they started burning, I made them stay open.

It made my skin hurt, and I could barely breathe.
I hugged Annabelle so close that I could
hear her whisper,

"It's ok to be afraid. I'm a bit afraid too! It's very dark when the lights are off. It's scary when the walls make funny sounds. But there is nothing under the bed in the dark that's not there in the light. There's nothing in the closet in the dark that's not there in the light. It's ok to be afraid when the lights are off.

You can be afraid; sometimes your skin hurts, your tummy feels sick, and your eyes burn. It's ok to feel afraid but don't let it have any power. Don't let fear stay. Have courage. You are stronger than your fear.

Fear can visit you, but do not let it move in."

You own your fear~ your fear doesn't own you.

I felt afraid for a few more minutes because the dark was still there, but I told fear it couldn't stay. I told fear it couldn't be stronger than me.

I pulled the blankets over my head and held Annabelle closer. I took a deep breath, let it out real slow, and pretended I was pushing the fear out with breaths.

I imagined fear like a feather going over a waterfall. Compared to the waterfall, the feather had no power. Compared to the truth, fear had no power either.

It took a lot of breaths, but Annabelle finally fell asleep.
If she could fall asleep, so could I.
If she could be courageous, then I could be, too.
Very quietly, I sang the happiest song I knew and took
my power back. Fear couldn't have it.

I *chose* to have courage.
I *chose* to rest and believe the truth.
I *chose* to believe that nothing was in my closet in the
dark that wasn't there in the light.

I said,

"Fear, you cannot stay.
You visited my soul, but now it's time to go."

Goodbye, FEAR.

i am JEALOUS

I was so jealous! My cousin got a puppy. I wanted a puppy. I told her a million trillion bazillion times I wanted a puppy, and I was going to name her Sophie the Marvelous. I begged my dad for a puppy, but he said I wasn't old enough to care for one. My cousin is younger than me, but her dad let her get a puppy.
And guess what she named it?

My cousin named her puppy Sophie the Marvelous!

I didn't want to play with my cousin anymore because we'd have to play with Sophie the Marvelous, and I wanted Sophie the Marvelous to belong to me.

She had a puppy, and I didn't.
When I went home, Sophie the Marvelous wouldn't come with me, because she wasn't mine. My cousin got what I wanted, and I was jealous. I didn't want to be her friend anymore. My insides were all twisted up like a knot because I was so jealous.
Maybe that was what jealousy looked like—
a twisted-up messy knot.
Annabelle held my hand and whispered to me.

"It's ok to feel jealous—for a minute. Someone got what you wanted. That's hard. You can play with Sophie the Marvelous, love her, and cuddle her. Maybe your cousin thought that if you weren't allowed to have Sophie the Marvelous, she would get her so you could still love the puppy.

You don't know why, so don't try to guess.

Think the best things, not the worst. Thinking the worst things gives jealousy power. Don't let jealous be more powerful than you. Be happy that you can see Sophie the Marvelous sometimes. Sometimes is better than not at all. Think of all the fun you and your cousin will have with Sophie the Marvelous. Being jealous will steal your friendship. Being jealous will hurt you, your cousin, and Sophie the Marvelous. It's not worth it.

Jealousy can't have power. Jealousy is a thief.
It steals everything and tells lies.
Jealousy can visit you, but do not let it move in."

You own your jealous— your jealous doesn't own you.

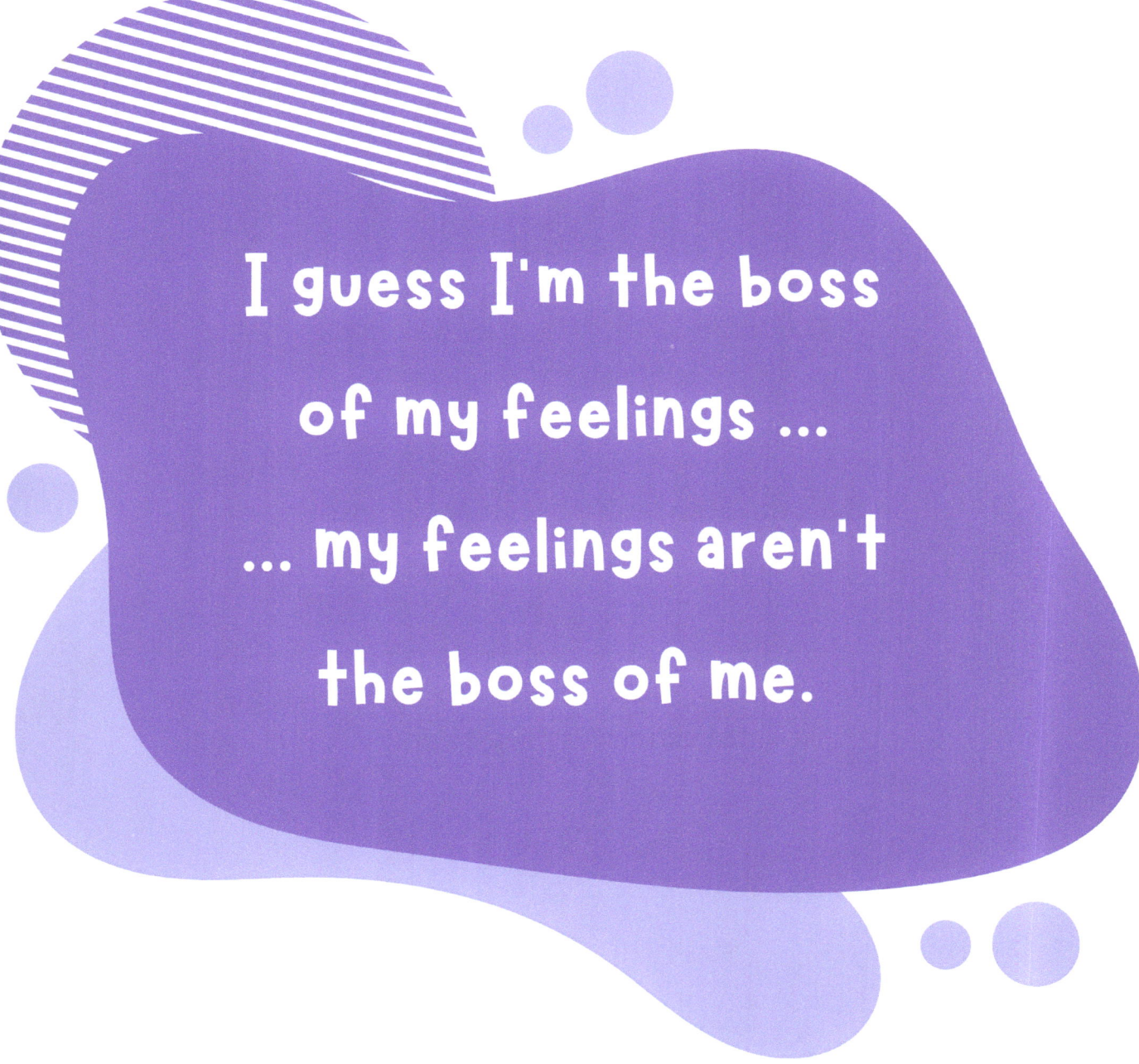

Annabelle was right.
It was better to love Sophie the Marvelous some of the
time than not at all.
I didn't know why my cousin got a puppy.
I didn't know why she named the puppy
Sophie the Marvelous.

I guess I didn't need to know everything. It wouldn't
make a difference since jealousy couldn't stay.
It couldn't have power.

I swung Annabelle around and started singing
the happiest song I knew.

I forgave my cousin for having what I wanted. I forgave her for naming the puppy Sophie the Marvelous. I closed my eyes and dreamed of one day having my own puppy but for now, I would play with her puppy.

I *chose* to be ok with that.
I *chose* to let that be enough.
I *chose* to be happy for her and happy for me.
I chased jealousy away because keeping it was not good for me. It couldn't be stronger than me.

"Jealous-you cannot stay.
You visited my heart, but now it's time to go."

Goodbye, JEALOUS.

i am LONELY

Oh, I was so lonely.

It made my heart hurt quite a lot.
My cousin had Sophie the Marvelous to play with.
My friend Violet was busy with Genevieve.
My dad was working in the shop.
Annabelle was getting her bow fixed, and Mom said my dolly had to go into the wash. I had nobody to play with, and I felt lonely.

It felt a little like sadness and a little like madness, but different, like a piece of me was missing, or lost, or sleeping. Like I was all alone in the great big world.

It whispered lies like, "You're not important."

There were lots of things I could do. I liked to draw, or I could play with my other toys. I didn't like playing alone, though; I was thinking about how lonely I was. The more I thought about it, the lonelier I felt.

I wished I had Annabelle to tell me what to do. But I supposed if I had Annabelle, I wouldn't be lonely.

I sat down on my bed to think about how lonely I was.

Instead, I started to wonder about Annabelle and what she might say. She was very wise, Annabelle was. She knew things I didn't know about feelings and power and what was true and what was not true.

She taught me to tell my feelings to leave me alone, and how to keep my power.

I wish everyone could have an Annabelle.

Oh, how I missed her. Oh, how lonely I felt without her.

Annabelle would probably say:

"It's ok to be lonely. I'm lonely, too. When you're all alone, and it hurts your heart, you must let it feel hurt for a little while, but don't let it have any power.
It can feel like you'll be alone forever, but you won't.
It feels like you're not important, but you are.
It feels like you don't matter, but you do.
It can feel like you're a little lost, but you're not.

It's ok to feel lonely—but not forever. Don't let lonely be more powerful than you.

Loneliness can visit you, but do not let it move in."

**You own your lonely~
your lonely does not own you.**

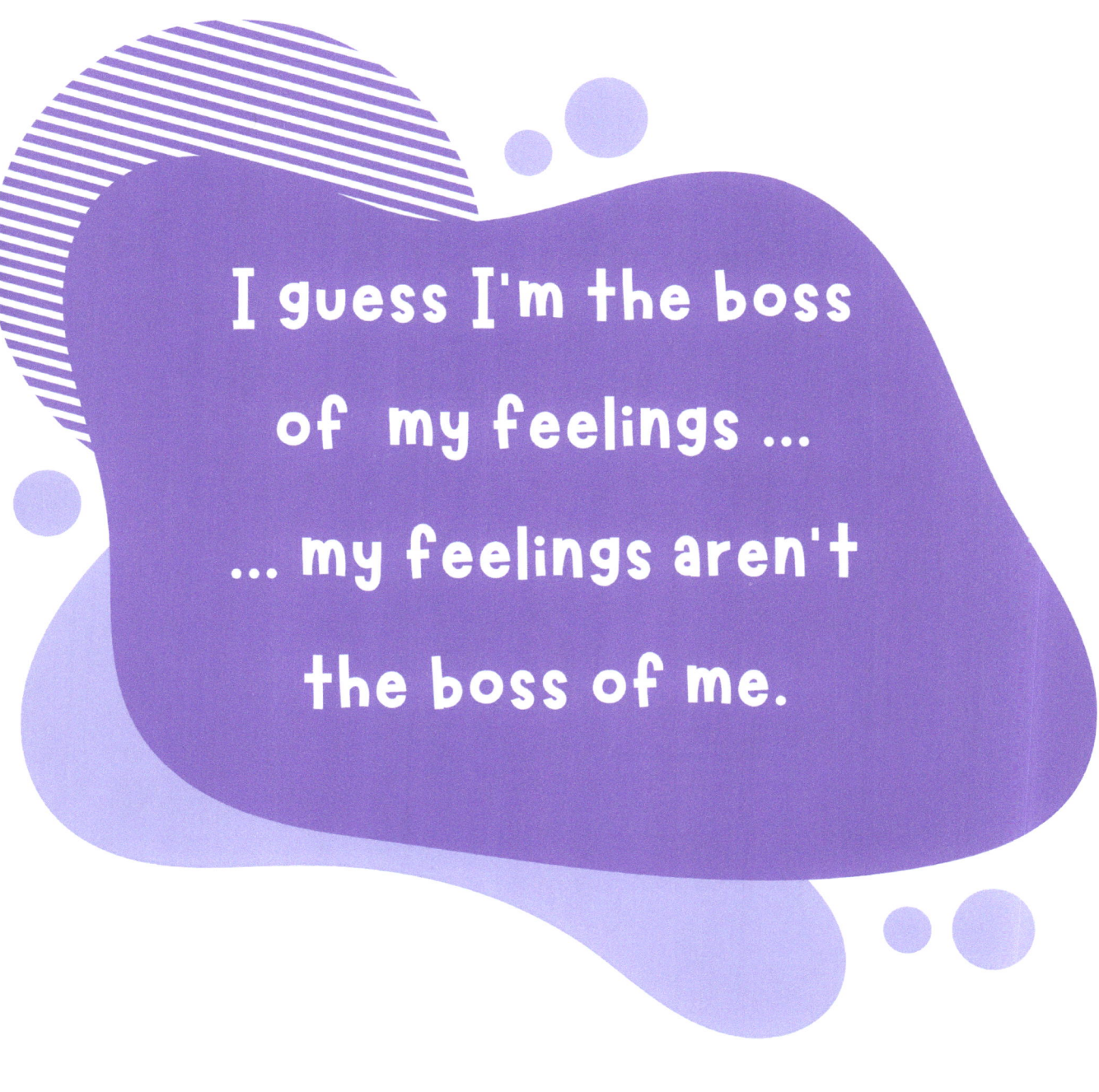

I let myself feel lonely for a few more minutes, but then I chased it away. The longer I let it stay, the harder it was to make it go. The longer it whispered to me, the more power it had. Instead, I thought about all the people who loved me. Just because they were away didn't mean they didn't love me.
They were just busy today, and that was ok.

I decided to play make-believe with my other toys; I played with Annabelle so much I wondered if other toys felt lonely, too. We played tea party and hide-and-seek. We told secrets and giggled.
I noticed the lonely was gone.
It couldn't stay forever.
It had no power.

"Lonely, you cannot stay. You visited my heart, but now it's time to go."

Goodbye, Lonely.

i am HAPPY

I felt so happy; I could sing and dance all day. Maybe I would.
Not everything was perfect.
Annabelle lost a shoe, and her hair was all tangled, but she was still beautiful.
Violet moved away, so I didn't get to see her anymore, but I'd make some new friends. Genevieve was nice.

I still didn't have a puppy named Sophie the Marvelous.
Before I went to sleep, I checked my closet and under my bed, because I knew the truth was that there was nothing in the dark that wasn't there in the light.

I still get so SAD that I sometimes cry, but that's ok.
It's ok to cry.
I sometimes get so MAD that it feels like my head might explode.
Once in a while, I get very JEALOUS, but not enough to give it any power.
Last week, I felt LONELY when Annabelle had to go in the wash, but I played with other things.
I am not happy because everything is perfect. I am happy because Annabelle taught me how to be happy. She taught me how to have power over my feelings and choose which ones get to stay and which ones have to leave.
I still feel my feelings when they come because they are important.
But I don't give them any power, and they cannot stay.

I am happy because I choose to be happy.

I wish everyone could have an Annabelle. She is very wise.

So, I *choose* to be HAPPY.
I *choose* to be kind because being kind is important.
I *choose* to sing the happiest song I know, no matter what my heart feels like, and I dance all over the room with sweet Annabelle.
I am proud that I learned not to give away my power.
I am glad I learned I was in charge of my feelings.

I learned it is good to feel our feelings, think about them, and understand them. Sometimes, our thoughts tell us lies and try to convince us to let bad feelings stay. Sometimes, the feelings don't want to go. But we must chase them away so the good feelings can come.
.
Happy and sad can't stay at the same time for long.

We must choose one or the other.

It's our *choice*.
We must think about our feelings but not let our feelings tell us how to think.

We are courageous when we chase negative feelings away.
We are wise when we choose good feelings even though the negative ones want to stay.

We are brave when we apologize.
We are even more brave when we forgive.
We are the most brave when we forgive people who aren't sorry.

Be courageous. Be wise. Be brave.

**It's ok to cry.
So cry if you must,
but don't cry forever.**

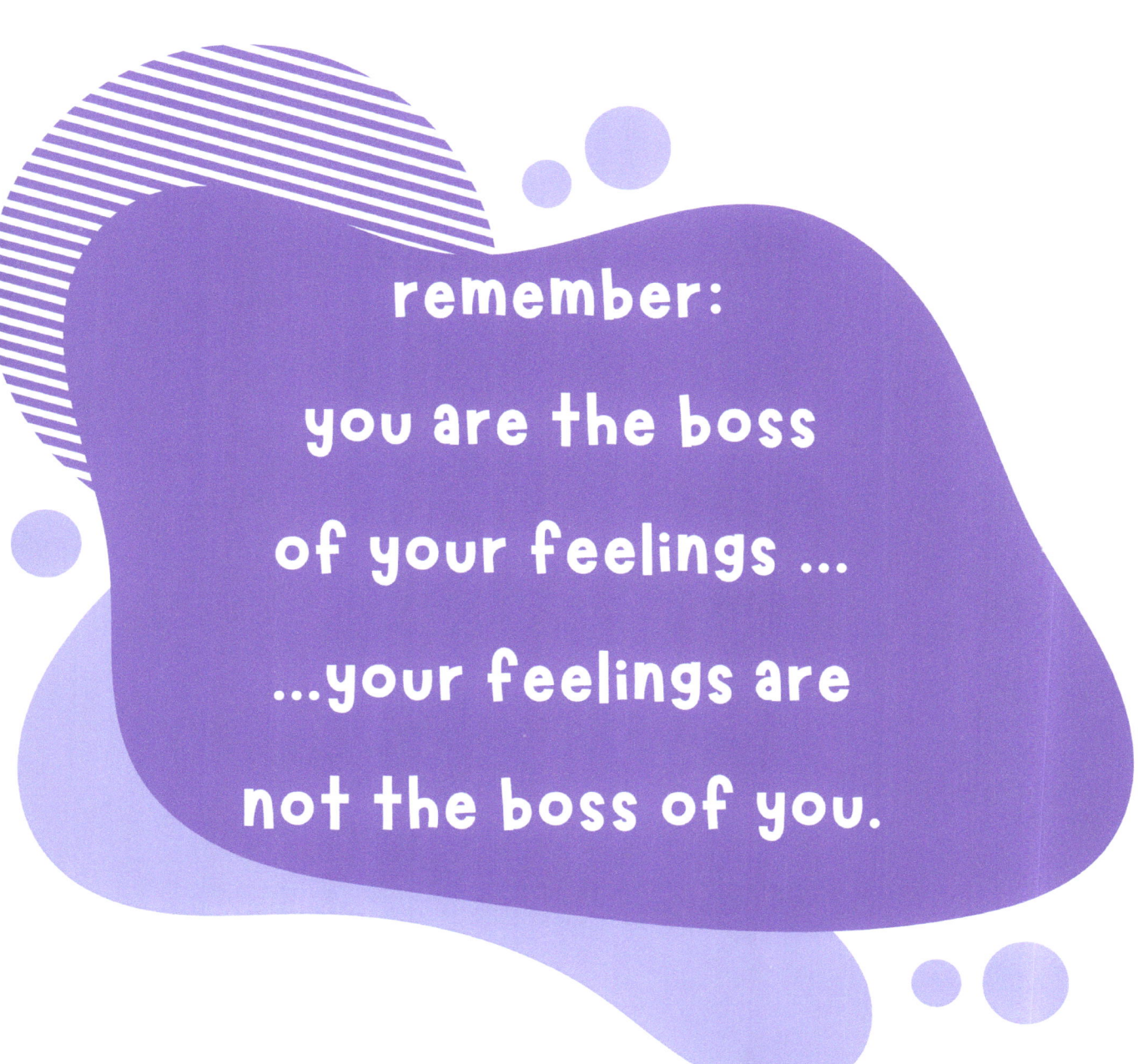

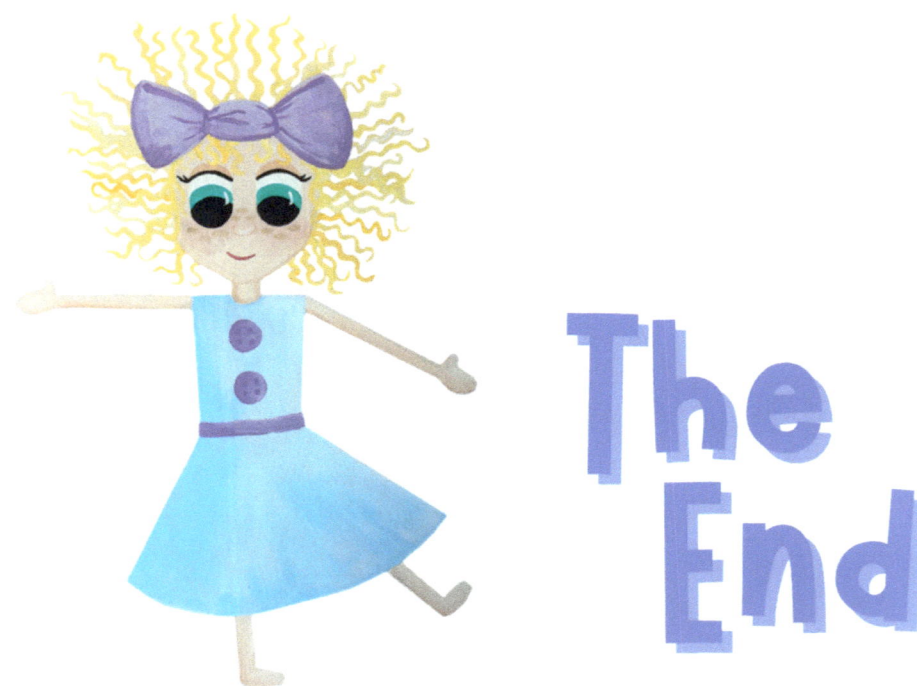